A CAT IN THE FAMILY
A Quarterly

By Uschi Birr
Translated by U. Erich Friese

INTRODUCTION

We are beholden to FALKEN-VERLAG GmbH., 65527 Niedernhausen/Ts., Germany for allowing us to translate this book from the original German. The German title is *Die Katze in der Familie*, which we translated as *A Cat in the Family*. The author, Uschi Birr, is a very famous lady in Germany. She is the Chief Editor for the leading pet magazine in Germany (*Ein Herz fuer Tiere*), which might well be the largest circulation pet magazine in the world. She is also a television personality and has kept cats since she was a little girl.

WHAT IS A QUARTERLY?

Keeping cats and kittens as pets is a rapidly expanding hobby. It is estimated that 100 million families in the English-speaking world keep a cat as a pet. With such a huge following, the science of keeping cats advances quickly. Consequently there is a need for rapid dissemination of knowledge at the lowest possible price. For this reason, this quarterly is being published in both magazine format and hard-cover format. Publishers of magazines are accustomed to bringing out their publications quickly. Thus the information in a magazine is more up-to-the-minute than the information in most books. Naturally, the price of the hard-cover edition is higher than the magazine edition. Both editions are brought to you at a very low price because of the support of advertisers.

PHOTOGRAPHY: The author wishes to thank the following people for allowing their photos to be used in this book: Reinhard Tierfoto, Archiv fuer Kunst und Geschichte, Bild-Agentur Geduldig, Bildagentur IPO, W.P. Mara, P.U.Pinzer, Ralf Ziegler, Manfred Ruckzip, Pussy-Versand, H.- J. Schwartz, Margrit Stueber, Isabelle Francais, Gillian Lisle, and Robert Pearcy.

yearBOOKS, INC.
Dr. Herbert R. Axelrod,
  Founder & Chairman
Neal Pronek
  Chief Editor

yearBOOKS are all photo composed, color separated, and designed on Scitex equipment in Neptune, N.J. with the following staff:

DIGITAL PRE-PRESS
  Michael L. Secord
    Supervisor
  Robert Onyrscuk
  Jose Reyes

COMPUTER ART
  Sherise Buhagiar
  Patti Escabi
  Sandra Taylor Gale
  Pat Marotta
  Joanne Muzyka

  Advertising Sales
George Campbell
  Chief
Amy Manning
  Director

©yearBOOKS,Inc.
1 TFH Plaza
Neptune, N.J. 07753
Completely manufactured in Neptune, N.J.
USA

This two-month-old mixed breed kitten is ready to go to its new home.

CONTENTS

American Shorthair shaded silver queen and her kittens.

Friends...Contrary to popular belief, cats and dogs can get along well together if they are introduced while they are both young.

HISTORY: FROM WILD CAT TO DOMESTICATED PET

To this day, science is uncertain as to when and how the cat became a domesticated animal. Only "where" this process took place has been firmly established, together with the fact that the domestication of the cat—in contrast to all other domesticated animals—extended over a period of thousands of years. The cat was not forced into the service of man as a "useful" captive animal, but instead sought out the proximity of man quite willingly as a follower of human culture. The cat resembled those animals (such as pigeons, swallows, and mice) that derive

As the popularity of cats as pets has increased, more data has been gathered on their social development and behavior patterns.

The cat as mythological symbol—the embodiment of the Egyptian goddess Bastet (6 B.C.).

substantial survival benefits from human civilization. Essentially, they prefer to establish themselves within human habitation, without becoming effectively domesticated.

The cat joined the household of man only about 8,000 years ago, tolerated as a participant in human culture because it caught mice. Presumably this first contact took place in the region known today as Abu Simbel (Egypt), when man first settled there. He was then joined by the shy, nocturnal African wild cat (*Felis sylvestris libyca*), a solitary animal that decimated the mice plague in food storage facilities. The first

graphical depictions of cats come from that era. It is estimated that the cat was first tamed approximately 2,500 BC and became actually domesticated about 1,000 years later. At about that time, the cat became a mythical symbol in Egypt. Popular belief had it that all cats had god-like qualities, and so man revered the cat accordingly.

Not only the descendants of the Nubian pale yellow (fallow) cat were kept in temples. During the peak of the rule of the Pharaohs (during the second millennium BC), the jungle cat (*Felis chaus*) was also kept. However, these must have been individual animals only, because the majority of pictorial representations, which document the early history of cats in association with man, clearly show descendants of the Nubian pale yellow (fallow) cat (a subspecies of the European wild cat).

It must have been this cat that migrated from Egypt a few centuries later. As this cat was initially an animal with a god-like status and was under the protection of priests, the state and the people, every effort was made to prevent it from leaving Egypt. Smuggling cats—as well as killing cats—incurred the death penalty. In spite of such draconian measures, the first cats reached Palestine as early as 1,700 BC and Crete a little later—presumably via traveling merchants. There, they were neither pets nor mouse catchers but instead were regarded as exotic, mysterious animals. Neither the Greeks nor the Romans really knew what to do with them. Later, the reaction of the Indians was very similar when the first cats arrived in Asia about 200 BC, again brought there by traveling merchants. In the fifth Century BC, the cat became established in southern Italy and in Greece. With its adaptability and fertility, the cat managed to survive there for nine centuries. By 400 AD, the Romans had learned to appreciate the cat as a useful mouse catcher, rather than as a cult animal. Things were different in Japan and China, where cats had arrived either via Indian or European merchants. The Chinese worshipped the "Holy Mao," which kept their country free of rats and mice, and they feared the female demon "Miai-Kui," which could cast spells on humans. The Japanese had ambivalent feelings toward the cat. On one hand, the monstrous "Nekomata" did her mischief; but on the other, the good fairy "Neko" brought blessings to every household. In order to elude Nekomata, people started to cut off the tail of all of these cats as early as 1,000 AD, and a distinct preference developed for kittens with a degenerated tail. The most beautiful "Nekos," the cats that would bring luck—tri-colored and with a "bob" tail—were reserved for the Emperor and his court. During the 11th Century, cats were given as presents to newly wedded couples as a good-luck charm, and they have held that role in some parts of the world to this very day.

At the end of the 9th Century AD, cats finally became parts of the daily life throughout Europe and Asia: they were adored, loved, used, endured, or viewed suspiciously, but not persecuted. That, however,

These kittens exhibit the curious, attentive nature characteristic of all cats.

changed with the spread of Christianity. As well as rejecting all pagan deities and customs, the early Christians also reviled the cat as a pagan fertility symbol. Cats, especially black ones, were considered to be the embodiment of the devil, and so they were made universal scapegoats, the cause of any bad luck, disease, war, or bad harvests. An unprecedented, relentless persecution of cats followed. Throughout Europe, hundreds of thousands of cats were tortured, mutilated, burned, and stoned to death.

The religious persecution of cats had far-reaching consequences. Because most cats had been exterminated (those that managed to survive withdrew into the vast forest areas still in existence in those days), rat and mouse populations increased unchecked. This then lead to the outbreak and very rapid spread of the fatal epidemic, the Black Death. This plague took the lives of millions of people. During those disease-ridden centuries, the cat in Europe remained an animal to be abused, at least by city people. Only gradually did cats return to the palaces and homes of nobility, but this time as pets for women. Eventually, cats were also tolerated on farms again.

In modern times, the cat was treated very differently in America than in western and central Europe. In the New World, cats were initially appreciated again as mouse catchers, because the cats on the ships of the pilgrims kept the ships free of rats. The first farmers regarded cats enthusiastically as useful domesticated animals; and in

Male cats in particular are very territorial animals. This cat has an unusually distinctive agouti coloration, which is more commonly seen in small mammals such as rodents and rabbits.

the cities, specially-bred, large specimens achieved record prices. These cats would not only keep houses free of rodent pests but also provided the pioneer women with companionship. Consequently, cats in the United States became pets much earlier than in Europe. Only the spread of industrialization, together with the increasing alienation of man from nature and the decline of the size of the family, influenced the cat's new status in Europe. Domesticated animals assumed the role of pets, with the primary purpose of providing company for man. England, already famous for its horse and dog breeding, was the first country with specific cat breeding to establish new varieties that conformed to the aesthetic desires of their owners. More and more new breeds were developed—a trend which is continuing to this day.

Two-month-old Exotic Shorthair kitten.

FROM KITTEN TO ADULT CAT

Irrespective of whether it is a pedigreed animal or simply a field-and-garden variety puss, whether it came from an animal shelter or from a farmyard, or whether it was born in someone's home, the important stages in the life of a cat are always the same. We humans must understand and appreciate what takes place in the course of a cat's life, because only then can we really comprehend the actions and reactions of cats.

DEVELOPMENT IN NEWBORN KITTENS

Warmth, security, and nest odor are the first things a newly born kitten perceives. It is, however, blind, and its hearing is poor. But it is the tactile (touch) sense, which has already developed 40 days prior to birth, that makes the kitten aware of the proximity of its mother and siblings. This particular sense acts like a thermometer, which is absolutely vital for the animal, because it is not yet capable of regulating its own body temperature. Such a young animal will instinctively crawl in the direction of warmth, on shaky legs and with awkward movements, but at least already in an upright position. The nose, fully functional from the first day, picks up the nest odor; and the brain will store it for the rest of the animal's life.

From day one, the kitten can distinguish its mother and siblings from other cats. Because such a young kitten cannot yet properly vocalize, its moaning call (the only sound a newborn kitten can make) is soft and barely audible. Nevertheless, the keen ear of the mother will hear it immediately. Moreover, she rarely ever leaves her litter during the first eight days. She spends about 70 percent of her time nursing the kittens; and if she does move away, she will immediately return once she hears the contact vocalization of the kittens.

A nursing female will defend her young literally to the last drop of her blood. Even to superior enemies, she will not surrender and is always ready to fight. Indeed, after the birth of the kittens, her flight readiness is blocked

Mixed breed queen and kitten. Kittens are highly dependent upon their mothers until they are weaned, which begins at about twenty-one days of age.

for about eight weeks.

The kittens are able to purr about 25 hours after birth; and from the fifth day on, their ears will turn toward unfamiliar sounds. They will be particularly alert to scratching noises, that is those that will later on in the life of the kitten trigger the hunting instinct.

But the most important of all senses that a cat possesses, sight, is the last one to become active. Not until one week after birth (over a two-to-three day period) will the eyes open. After about a month, kittens start to see clearly, but full visual perception is not fully developed until separation from the mother.

Almost there...Still on shaky legs, the baby cat crawls to its mother.

Seeing is not particularly important in these first few weeks, because kittens do little else around the clock than sleep and nurse. The mother stimulates her kittens, and after each meal she massages the stomach region of each of her young with her tongue, until proper digestion occurs. Milk from the female provides the young with essential nutrients and minerals required for proper development of muscles, bones, and tissue. Moreover,

they are "immunized" against all diseases with which the mother has come into contact. She passes the stored defensive substances (antibodies) via her milk to her offspring. The kittens are then protected against some of the most common infections, provided the kittens keep nursing.

The kittens do not become fully active until the beginning of the third week. At that stage they are able to distinguish between familiar and unfamiliar sounds, and they recognize the direction from which such acoustic signals are coming. The vocalizations become stronger and the "vocabulary" more comprehensive. Apart from the "scared" call for the mother, the kittens can now purr contentedly, give off a begging "meow," or even an annoyed chirp toward brother or sister. The mother, the siblings, and the nest, as well as familiar animals and humans, actually take on shape: the kittens now visually recognize these stimuli and move actively toward them. But because vision is not yet totally accurate in kittens at that age, their movements are still somewhat clumsy; and they have a tendency to trip and stumble during their early attempts to move about.

At this stage, the mother shows the first signs of exhaustion. She moves away every two to three hours for a few minutes, in order to groom herself, to stretch out and then recuperate. But she does not let her young out of her sight, and at the slightest alarm signal she returns immediately.

If a stranger approaches the litter, the kittens will hiss at him. With their first needle-sharp teeth (dentition is already complete after 5 weeks), the kittens will aggressively bite when they feel threatened and are without protection from the mother. Access to the milk source has given rise to a hierarchy. Each kitten in a litter has a teat, whereby the strongest young occupy the most advantageous location. Although the female continues to make sure that all of her kittens can digest properly, she no longer has to induce them to nurse. Now the kittens experience the feeling of hunger and will directly head for the teat. With their paws (in accordance with their particular respiratory and cardiac rhythm, respectively), they tap against the abdominal region of the female in order to stimulate the flow of milk.

THE LEARNING PHASE

During their second and third months, kittens enter a learning phase. During this period, they sleep little, something that is never to occur again their entire life; and they learn everything they need to know to survive in life. Most of this education takes place in the form of "play": they practice stalking, crouching, arching their back, evaluating whether a particular prey can be handled or not, jumping, pursuing, and escaping. The siblings play along as "prey," "hunter," "rivals," and "partners".

Their sense of balance and their muscles are being developed during climbing and

Not that simple, this balancing on a garden fence gate, but with some practice it can easily be done!

balancing. Thanks to the so-called vestibular position reflex, with which every kitten is born, no injury is sustained during risky jumps This reflex assures that when falling, the body is automatically put in an upright position, so that a cat always lands on all four feet simultaneously.

Failures in such daring ventures are equally undramatic, as is hunting in vain for imaginary or real prey. After all, the kittens are still under the protection of their mother, and her milk supply is occasionally still available to them. At times, she will become increasingly impatient with her "children," snapping at them when they seek body contact. But she is still there for them when danger threatens and will then gather the kittens around her. Moreover, she continues to be their role model: by watching her and imitating her, the kittens learn to defecate and urinate in the litter box. They also copy the female's stretching as well as the sharpening of the claws. They will also learn to distinguish between friend and foe, and between food that is poisonous and food that can be tasty.

When, about 12 weeks after birth, the female virtually ignores her young and keeps them away by hissing at them, the kittens are then physically and emotionally fit for a life on their own. At that point, the youngsters will become truly independent.

MATING

Young cats joining such firmly established "clans," have to prove themselves before they are accepted by

Birds of prey represent a deadly danger for young cats in the wild.

the other animals. The first few weeks of the year is the period of considerable antagonistic actions between cats (the mating instinct awakes as the days get longer). Sexually active males look for females that are ready to mate, and so they often enter other territories, which usually leads to fierce fighting. In order to attract females and to keep other males away, established males mark the borders of their territory with urine. Everybody knows the dreadful mating calls; they are supposed to be audible over great distances in order to attract females. Females in heat mark the area just like males and also attempt to attract them with calls. Because the calls of a female in heat will attract all males in the general area, her small territory will quickly turn into a battlefield. The female will specifically select a particular male as a mate.

The main mating season for wild cats is March, and in May about a third of all kittens are born. Males have to approach a female in heat cautiously and with considerable skill: even though the female is attempting to attract a male by rolling on her back and vocalizing, she will also hiss at him angrily when he attempts to jump on top of her. Immediately after copulation, the female turns ferocious; and a male that does not leap to safety quickly and with agility, may incur severe injuries. During the time that a female is in heat, she may copulate up to 20 times, enduring the firm neck bite that is used by the male to hold the female down. After

Two sexually active tomcats fighting over their territorial claims.

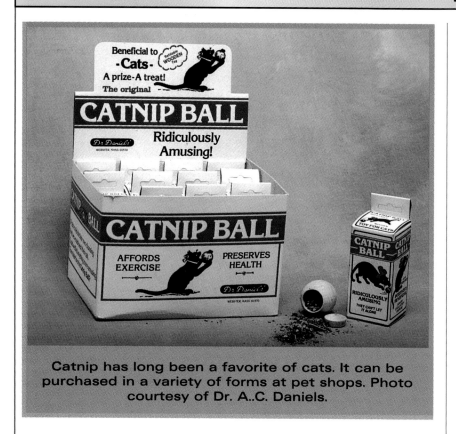

Catnip has long been a favorite of cats. It can be purchased in a variety of forms at pet shops. Photo courtesy of Dr. A..C. Daniels.

the mating season, females and males go their separate ways again.

While males tend to enter a resting period with lots of sleep after the mating season, the females start looking for a suitable nesting area, in a cave where the animal can not be disturbed and near rich hunting grounds. Females will now hunt and stray more than ever before, because their instincts tell them to build up their body fat reserve. Through continuous inspections of the territory around the future nesting site, the female will recognize any dangers as early as possible. All pregnant females look for a substitute nest where they can take their kittens if the first nest proves to be unsafe.

The week prior to the birth of her kittens, the female spends a great deal of time sleeping. Only after the young are eight days old will the female start to hunt again. Once the kittens have become independent, estrus will set in again and efforts for a new generation begin. Cats maintain their territory for about eight years and rear one or two litters per year before old age begins.

LONGEVITY OF CATS

A wild cat without human support and veterinary care can live about 15 years. Improved nutrition and veterinary care for domesticated cats have extended their longevity, so that 20-year-old animals are no longer an exception.

Old age begins rather early for a cat. From its ninth year onward the cat becomes increasingly sedate. There are few litters, and she avoids hostile interactions with other cats. The eyes are losing acuity, and the effectiveness of nose and ears also starts to decline. The joints are starting to show wear and tear. The active periods during the day become shorter and less frequent; older cats may sleep up to 20 hours per day. The need for warmth increases. Older cats like to lay in the sun, and at night they are looking for comfortable sleeping quarters. They are reluctant to go out hunting on very cold and wet days.

The immune system becomes weaker from about the thirteenth year onward. Viral and fungal infections are among the most common causes of death among old, wild cats, which have reduced immunity against such diseases. Because these animals have lost the strength to search for food, they will invariably die in their sleep; this is the reason why many people believe a cat knows when death is near and therefore goes into hiding.

Even cats kept in an apartment will age increasingly from their thirteenth year onward. Externally, this is visible only by a few white hairs on the face of the animal, and sometimes the eyes will become slightly clouded. The need for sleep, as well as for "snuggling up," increases with advancing age. Many house cats die of a stroke or of cardiac failure, or they are put down by a veterinarian once fatal tumors have been detected.

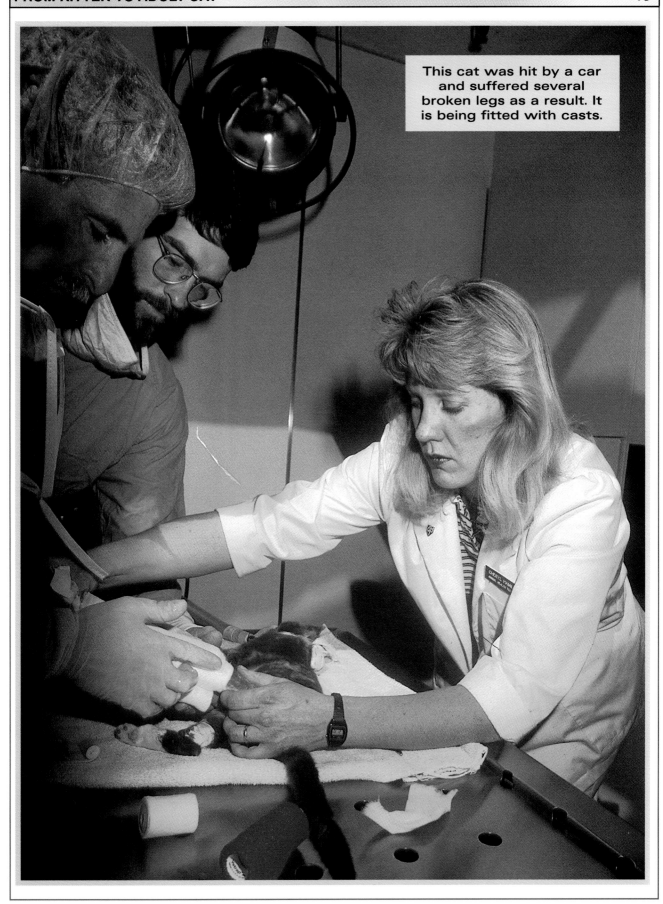

This cat was hit by a car and suffered several broken legs as a result. It is being fitted with casts.

Balinese kitten up a tree.
Domesticated cats are good at
climbing, jumping, and sprinting.

THE CAT'S BODY AND ITS CAPABILITIES

The cat is known as the most highly developed predator. Body and senses are—in our domesticated cat just as in its ancestors— perfectly equipped for hunting. small ground-dwelling prey.

A skeleton with more than 240 very light but strong bones and more than 500 muscles facilitate smooth, rapid movements. The flexible backbone can be bent into a U-shape, for instance when arching the back or during sleep. But the spine can also extend perfectly straight and even expand. The neck has similar flexibility. A cat can turn its head up to 180 degrees, for instance, for grooming purposes. This animal is quite capable of scratching behind its ears with one of the hind paws, and even cleaning the base of its tail with its tongue.

All cats are "toe walkers." When walking, they do not place the entire foot on the ground, only the pad. This extends the length of the legs and increases running speed. Cats have four pads each on the hind legs and five on each of the front legs. All are covered with a thick callused skin that affords an adequate grip when jumping or suddenly braking. Fat cells in the pads create a cushioning effect upon impact when jumping or during fast running. The pads also

provide a protective cover for a cat's most potent weapon: its sharp, bent claws. When the animal is running, the claws are kept within dermal pockets within the pads, by means of tendons on the toe muscles. Unlike the claws of dogs, those of cats are not in contact with the ground and so are not worn off; instead, this mechanism enables a

hunting cat to creep up silently on its prey. A cat looks after its claws meticulously. The front claws are sharpened daily by scratching on a tree trunk or some other solid material, sometimes also on walls. The hind claws are sharpened with the teeth during each grooming session. They are used mainly during climbing, while the larger and

The heavy musculature of the hind legs provides the strength needed for jumping—from a standing or sitting position. A healthy cat can jump over a distance five times its own body length.

stronger front claws are principally for defense and for grasping and holding prey. On the other hand, the muscles of the hind legs are nearly twice as heavy as those of the front legs. They indicate an enormous strength, mainly for jumping. From a standing or sitting position, a cat is quite

landing point, which is approached with sufficient thrust so that the rest of the way can be overcome by pulling the body up with the front claws. This is an extraordinary technique not found in any other climbing animal.

Although leaps onto

soundless stalking, lightning-fast prey capture, and their main weapons: their claws and teeth. For its size, the cat has the most potent "killer jaws" in comparison to all other terrestrial mammals.

The 30 teeth (fewer than in other carnivores) are located in short, highly movable jaws. Dentition consists of six tiny incisors (for grooming and trimming claws, as well as for light chewing) in upper and lower jaw, which are flanked on both sides by two dagger-like canine teeth on upper and lower jaw. These are used for grasping, holding and tearing the food apart. Toward the back of the jaws are grinding teeth (molar) in a scissor-like arrangement, used for cutting large food items into smaller pieces, which are easier to swallow. Adult cats possess two molars each in upper and lower jaw. There is room for a

Both of these photos show the enormous mobility of a cat's vertebral column; it can be contracted into a U-shape but can also be stretched totally horizontally.

capable of jumping forward, upward, sideways, and even backwards. To do that, it first pulls its knees and contracts its leg joints. This is followed by a lightning-fast body extension, which then creates sufficient thrust for the jump.

A healthy cat can jump over a distance five times its own body length, that is, without a running start. A cat will jump while in motion only if it knows exactly what its target is. On the other hand, new structural obstacles are first carefully evaluated. Height and distance are estimated, and the cat jumps off at the lowest possible angle to reach the target. In doing this, a cat always attempts to jump higher than the actual position of its target so that it lands on its hind legs, using the tail and front paws for balancing. If the distance is too far for a single leap, the cat will use an intermediate

obstacles up to six feet high do not pose any problem at all for cats, nearly all of them hesitate when they have to pass over a hurdle on which they cannot land. For instance, most would rather walk around a nine-inch-high fence, or simply try to climb over it. Also difficult for cats is the return from high places, because they shy away from jumping down or actually climb down head first. When cats need to be rescued from trees, they would rather stay aloft for days rather than risk the way down.

Although domesticated cats are good at climbing, jumping, and sprinting, they are not good at running long distances. A relatively small heart and the comparatively weak lungs will tire a running cat quickly. Consequently, cats invariable take an upward escape route. When hunting prey, cats rely on

The two canine teeth not only look dangerous...they are. They are used for grasping, holding, and tearing food apart.

total of six molars in the lower jaw and ten molars in the upper jaw. There are only 26 milk teeth, because the four lower molars are absent. Cats start to teeth from the third week after birth onward; the permanent teeth start to replace the milk teeth gradually from the 14th week onward.

THE SENSES

Many of the cat's extraordinary capabilities still remain to be explained scientifically, such as anticipating earthquakes and being able to find its way back home over great distances. In fact, the cat belongs to those exceptional creatures whose five senses are optimally developed. The interaction between visual acuity, perfect hearing, delicate nose, tactile capability, and sense of taste makes for a far more diverse world for these four-legged creatures than for us humans.

VISION

The shiny cat eye, which glows intensively at night, is particularly conspicuous. The pupil can narrow down to a millimeter-wide slot, as well as

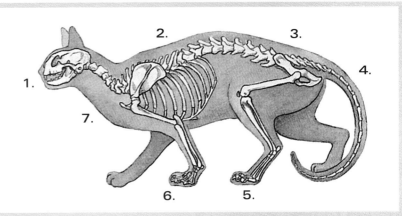

Skeleton: 244 bones
Muscles: 512
Weight: 6-12 pounds
1. Permanent dentition: 30 teeth
2. Thorax: 13 vertebrae
3. Pelvis: 7 vertebrae
4. Tail: 20-23 vertebrae
5. Hind toes and claws: 4 each
6. Front toes and claws: 5 each
7. Neck: 7 vertebrae

Cat anatomy at a glance. The average weight for a cat is between 6 to 12 lbs. The overall length of the body is about 1½ feet.

expands when the animal is scared, in pain, stressed, or in shock. The eyes as such are relatively rigid: they can not be rolled or moved in their sockets. The animal compensates for this with its extremely flexible neck;

Left: The large shiny eyes, with pupils that can contract to a narrow slit, are the most conspicuous feature of a cat. Right: When the nictitating membrane is constantly visible, a veterinarian must be consulted because this can be a symptom of a serious disease.

expand into an eye-filling disk. The eyes reflect not only the light intensity, but also display the mood of a cat. Just as in humans, whose eyes darken when a person is sad or frightened, a cat's pupil

instead of having to move the eyes, the cat simply turns its head. The movable upper and stationary lower lid protect the eye ball against injuries from foreign bodies. A third lid, the so-called nictitating

membrane, prevents the eye from drying out. This lid is located in the inner corner of the eye, and it supplies the eye with sufficient tear liquid. Therefore, unlike humans, cats do not have to blink their eyes every few seconds. Blinking is used deliberately and purposely by cats; it is simply part of their body language. The nictitating membrane has yet another protective function: it wipes dust particles away. Normally, the third lid is retracted into the corners of the eyes. A constantly visible nictitating membrane indicates not only the presence of an eye disease but can also be symptomatic of other internal diseases. When this occurs, it is advisable to consult a veterinarian.

In domesticated cats, the iris shimmers amber-yellow to pale green. In pedigreed cats, the iris can be blue, turquoise, jade-green, golden, orange, or copper-red. Even two different colors may occur simultaneously in the same animal. The reason for such a colorful spectrum is the embedded color pigments. In newborn kittens with incomplete pigmentation, the iris is bluish-gray with a metallic sheen up to the 12th week after birth. This is gradually replaced with the permanent color of the iris. Visual acuity, however, is not being influenced at all by the color of the iris. It has a different task: light-sensitive

A good close-up of the sensory hairs, or whiskers, on the face of a cat. The hairs are embedded in vascularized sacs that contain highly sensitive nerve fibers.

muscles contract with decreasing light levels and so create more space for the pupil and the (internal) retina. On the other hand, under extreme brightness (direct sun light), these muscles expand to such an extent that only a very small segment of the pupil remains visible.

A cat can see everything that takes place in front of it and sideways up to an angle of 180 degrees. Vision is three dimensional, just as in humans, and consequently a cat estimates precisely the distance and shape of an object. Over very short distances cats are far sighted, and over longer distances they are near sighted.

A cat's world does not present itself as colorfully as ours. Cats can distinguish between blue and green, black and white, but cannot differentiate yellow, orange, and red. However, this color blindness has certain advantages. The surface of the retina has 25 times as many light-sensitive rods as color-sensitive rods. These rods can collect remnant light rays during very low light levels. In addition, the pupil is opened up to a diameter of 12 mm, and all light rays that are not collected by the rods hit the mirror-like tissue layer behind the retina. This so-called *tapetum lucidum* ("shiny spot") reflects all light and so again stimulates the light- sensitive cells of the eye. This reflection of remnant rays causes the characteristic glow of cats' eyes at night. Due to this double-utilization of available light, cats can recognize shapes, outlines, and, of course, movements at night and during dusk and dawn.

TACTILE SENSE

Apart from protective wool and guard hairs, the cat's skin is covered by so-called sensory hairs, which are stiffer, longer, and stronger than the rest of the hairs making up the coat. The most conspicuous ones are the 30 or so "whiskers," located on the upper and lower lips, respectively. Next to them, on the cheeks there are two such hairs each, and above the eyes are about ten and on the back of the paws,

Cats investigate the shape and consistency of objects by pawing at them.

at the so-called carpal organ, there are about another five such hairs.

These sensory hairs are more than twice as thick as the coat hairs, and they are embedded three times as deep in the skin. Their roots are located in highly vascularized sacs with a multitude of sensory nerves and highly sensitive muscles. With the help of the latter, a cat can virtually turn the sensory hairs "on" and "off." In turn, the nerve fibers react sensitively to vibrations, temperature, and air pressure. This possibly explains why many cats register explosions many miles away, become restless when a thunderstorm approaches, and apparently can anticipate—days in advance—natural catastrophes such as floods, volcanic eruptions, cyclones, and earthquakes. All of these events set off vibrations, which are received by the tactile hairs. Usually, the tactile sense is used in order to determine the degree of danger from something unfamiliar. Anything new is observed initially very cautiously and from a safe distance. Then the cat raises its whiskers forward and fans them widely to test the temperature and consistency of the object. Only after such a perusal has been completed is the touch sense turned off, by returning the whiskers to their original position. The cat then concentrates on smell. Once this has been assessed, the touch sense is turned on once again, this time via the tactile hairs on the paws and above the nose. Both of them react to the slightest touch and report on shape and consistency of the object. This touching with the pads of a front paw can be observed in our house cats whenever they discover a new toy and keep "pawing" at it.

SENSES OF SMELL AND TASTE

Closely connected to the tactile sensors are the senses of smell and taste. The tactile nerves in the pads have pendants to the nasal speculum and to the tongue. Touching, smelling, and tasting are indeed interconnected in cats. The significance of the sense of smell is best documented by the fact that these animals use their nose just about anywhere at any time: before feeding, while defecating and urinating, when laying down, when playing, and particularly when interacting with other cats, other animals, or humans. 200 million olfactory cells located in the pharyngeal space between nose and gums filter various aromatic substances from the air and categorize them into important and unimportant. The olfactory nerves are strongly stimulated by smells from food and through sexual pheromones (aromatic substances) given off by other cats.

An unknown and extremely attractive aroma is tested by the cat opening both lips and drawing in air across the tongue, and pressing it against the gum (toward Jacob's Organ, a supplementary olfactory organ). This small cone-shaped organ enhances the detection of interesting odors and serves mainly to identify the chemical methods given off by other cats.

Since the sense of taste is initially stimulated by smell, a cat that has a cold will no longer feed or will take only foods that give off a strong odor. What has not yet been explained scientifically is the preference of all cats, irrespective of age, sex, and

Cats should never have access to houseplants as many of them are poisonous.

species (e.g., lions) for certain oils, such as valerian or catnip. Although the substance that triggers this behavior (nepetalactone) is known, its purpose is not understood. What is known is that cats smelling valerian or catnip start to salivate, roll on the ground, kick their legs, and maul objects with their

paws and teeth. The pet industry has taken advantage of this and offers toys scented with catnip. The sense of smell leads a cat to feed and drink and activates the taste nerves, which are located on the tip and base of the tongue, and along the lateral gum walls. With them, the cat distinguishes water quality, as well as salty, bitter, and spicy flavors. Sweet taste is not detected. The preference for milk and cream may be due to the fatty or sweetish odor, but certainly not because of the sugary taste. Indeed, for all food and drink the cat relies not on its tongue but instead on its nose.

HEARING

While the sense of smell plays an important role while feeding, it is hardly used for catching prey. Instead, when hunting, the cat relies on its eyes and extremely acute hearing, which in turn relate closely to the tactile sense of the animal. After all, sounds are nothing more than vibrations, which reach the tactile and the hearing organs. That also explains why cats prick up their ears before they actually perceive a sound. They put their ears in the "receive" mode, just like a satellite dish, because the tactile sense conveys to the animal that a message is coming. Both ears can be turned independently and up to an angle of 180 degrees toward the source of a sound. A cat not only hears sounds, but it can also identify them: where they are coming from, how far away the source is, and in which direction and with what speed the sounds are produced. For instance,

A cat has a keen sense of sight and a keen sense of hearing, qualities that easily enable it to detect prey.

when stalking prey in high grass, a cat can—on the basis of sound received—calculate where the prey must be before it actually leaps in that direction. Because all socially interactive rodents, such as field mice, communicate with family members with ultra-high chirping sounds, a cat finds their nests with its hearing and tactile senses alone. This occurs even when prevailing weather and light conditions render eyes and nose ineffective.

Hearing plays yet another important role. It also determines the "picture" a cat perceives of the world around it. Familiar sounds serve the cat for orientation and recognition of its territory. When homing in on its nest from a radial distance of up to three miles, the cat relies mainly on sound sources; their distance and direction indicate to the animal the shortest route to take. For example, when leaving the "nest," the animal's hearing establishes a sound image—water falling in the south, 500 yards away; traffic noise, one-half mile westward; leaves rustling, 100 yards north. If the cat suddenly gets lost, such as after a panic flight, the animal simply recalls these sound images. The cat then "searches" for a familiar sound, which it will encircle until other matching sounds, stored in its sound memory, are found.

Sound images also determine a cat's feeling for time. It will wait at specific times for the sound of the can opener, or it is right there when footsteps in the hallway announce the arrival of its master.

When climbing, a cat relies heavily on its front claws to pull itself upward. A cat will not hesitate to climb great heights but getting back down is another matter, which is why they sometimes have to be rescued.

Cats enjoy the company of their owners, but they can also be perfectly content spending some quiet time all by themselves.

THE CAT'S WORLD

Whenever a cat moves in or is taken in, it will establish its own world within a few days. It will set up a daily rhythm that will be difficult to break.

A cat's daily life consists of sleeping, eating, grooming, hunting and social contacts, interrupted only by inspection walks and leisure time. Whichever of these activities is prevalent depends on the time of year, the cat's physical constitution, and environmental conditions. In free-living cats, the biorhythm is determined by the time of day, season of the year, as well as by sex hormones. On the other hand, a family cat will soon adjust to the human activities around it. She adjusts play or hunting and contact periods to those times when the family is present, and spends the time when nobody is at home with sleeping and leisure hours. A cat's "home" is divided into sleeping, feeding, grooming, and toilet sites, which are all interconnected by established walking paths. When there are several cats under the same roof, each will have its own special places, which are vigorously defended against intruders (even against its own mate).

THE SLEEPER

As so much time is spent at them, sleeping sites are most important. With 14 to 18— even 20—hours of sleep a day, cats are the longest sleepers among mammals. They distribute sleeping periods over the entire day and so continuously interrupt all other activities. Genuine deep sleep, the so-called REM (rapid eye movements) phase, lasts six to seven minutes and occurs only during a few sleep periods. That is when cats are dreaming, which can be recognized by twitching limb movements. Yet the body is totally relaxed, and it is difficult to wake up the animal. When brought out of a deep sleep, the cat needs a little while to re-adjust. It could also retaliate with biting, scratching or hissing.

The small "naps," which last from 10 to 30 minutes,

A mixed breed kitten can make just as good a pet as the most expensive pedigreed kitten.

are actually dozing and resting with periods of light or semi-sleep, respectively. At that time, the senses operate only by "pilot light." Each key stimulus, such as opening a can, doors slamming, or a dog barking, will wake up the cat immediately. During extended sleeping periods, light sleep alternates with deep sleep. During intermediate stages of sleep, a cat may even get up and turn around on the spot a few times, before laying down again—similar to humans tossing and turning in their sleep.

Cats always have several sleeping sites. If possible, these are warm, protected, cave-like corners, which afford protection at the back and an adequate overview toward the front. Kittens and totally exhausted adult cats will simply "fall" into bed. Usually, however, bedding down is preceded by certain preparations, which may take a minute or two: superficial grooming, brief inspection or walking around the sleeping site, smelling the site, preliminary bedding down (trying different positions) and finally the first yawn, followed by a brief period of dozing. At that stage the animal keeps changing its position until it is finally comfortable and then falls asleep.

Normal waking up again takes a while. The muscles need to be loosened up, extensive yawning provides the circulatory system with plenty of oxygen and the animal becomes fully alert. Shaking her head slightly after getting up on her feet, the cat—standing on the tips of her toes on all four feet— arches her back. This is

Catnap. With about 14 to 18 hours of sleep daily, cats are the longest sleepers among mammals.

A cat has scent glands on various parts of its body, including its cheeks. This cat is marking its territory by rubbing its cheeks against the walkway.

followed by extending the front limbs far forward and at the same time de-arching her back, now pressing it firmly downward ,just as humans would stretch their entire body. Then the cat extends each hind limb separately, shakes her body briefly and prepares to face the world.

From the sleeping place there is usually a direct path to the feed dish and another one to the toilet. Other pathways lead to various vantage points.

GROOMING

Apart from those places where the cat rests or spends leisure time, the grooming sites are also important. A cat spends about two hours a day looking after its coat. In

The famous "cat wash" not only serves grooming purposes but also diffuses stress situations.

addition to a thorough cleaning, a cat will attend briefly—10 to 20 times a day—to its coat and skin; this is the often cited "cat wash."

This activity is not only for cosmetic purposes but also wets the coat when the animal is too hot. The evaporation of the saliva cools the skin. Because of this activity, cats tend to lose a lot of body fluid, which must be replenished by drinking. Therefore, it is important that there is always an adequate water supply available. The cat wash is also important in situations of conflict or under stress or when the cat is scared. Everyone knows the feeling of rising body heat when becoming angry or embarrassed. A cat compensates for any "feverish" excitement by a hectic wetting of its pelt.

Finally, grooming is also part of the pacification gesture in the repertoire of body language. The cat mother shows affection to her kittens in that way; members of the colony will groom each other in order to stop imminent fighting. This sort of "peace offering" can often be observed among two cats living in the same house. If both of them want to settle in the same location, they will quickly stare at each other. After a somewhat tense moment, one of the two will lower her head, and the other will briefly lick her head, and there is harmony again!

The main purpose of grooming, however, is taking care of the coat and skin. It involves using the tongue, teeth, paws and claws. The wide, but short, cat tongue has a rough surface created

by horny papillae. With it, even bones can be rasped clean. Therefore, a cat's gentle stroke over human skin can be a somewhat painful experience. But when these papillae are being stroked over the pelt, they remove dust, foreign particles, broken-off hairs, skin scales and excessive secretion. Firmly embedded clumps of dirt or

Being the adept hunter that it is, a cat will carefully fix in on its prey before leaping at it.

parasites are grasped with the cat's tiny, so-called flea teeth and are virtually nibbled out of the pelt. Each part of the body is carefully groomed with the tongue. Only the head requires some "outside help." Therefore, the cat then licks her paw and then wipes it across her face; five to ten times per grooming session. To remove tough, matted patches in the fur, the cat used the claws on the hind limbs. Cats wash themselves in any position, even while in motion.

COMMUNICATION

The original solitary cat has maintained part of its cool behavior toward other cats. Communication between several cats is largely via elements of smell. A cat that is self assured marks its sitting and feeding spots. It shows the other cats where its regular paths and territorial borders are, occupies hunting and sleeping sites and calmly covers over the marks left by brave intruders with its own marks. Even in households with more than one cat, each animal will mark each of its own corners and respects those belonging to the others.

Communication between two cats, such as during accidental encounters as well as during disputes, takes place with a combination of body and vocal languages. To cats, both of these are understandable, even over considerable distances. There is a deliberate ignoring, casually strolling past each other at a distance of at least three feet or more. This sort of behavior avoids actual fighting.

Cats do not often capture prey that is in flight.

Real confrontations are rare; and if they do occur, both combatants will try to decide the outcome of such fights without injuries. The actual fight is very short but intense. After a few seconds, both animals will break apart. The weaker one flees (and will not be followed by the other), or the threat behavior will start all over again.

Above: A cat fight about to start...For the most part, cat fights do not last long; but even so, they can result in considerable injury to either or both combatants. Below: Personality can vary noticeably in cats. Note the position of the ears on the orange and white cat: they are pointed back, an indication of aggressive behavior.

CARE AND MAINTENANCE

Before you bring your kitten home, you should have all of the furnishings and accessories that the newcomer will need. Doing so will make for a smooth transition for the new member of the family.

THE SCRATCHING POST

A scratching post is a "must" for all cats. Your pet will not only hone her claws on it but will also mark it as part of her territory. Therefore it should be situated in the direct pathway leading from the sleeping basket or site, because after a cat wakes up and has stretched herself, she will always walk the same path—either to her favorite spot in which she suns or grooms herself, or to the food bowl. The scratching post should be placed between these two points.

A scratching post is a must for every cat-owning household.

Pet shops offer scratching posts in a wide variety of models and sizes. A scratching post must be "scratch- friendly." That is, it must have a rough, fibrous surface. It should be high enough so that the cat can extend its front legs when it scratches.

A PLACE TO SLEEP

A favorite sleeping spot for any cat is always warm, protected, and located as high as possible, in any case, above floor level. The floor is used only for short dozing periods or for sunbathing. For extended periods of sleep, the cat will do the same thing its ancestors did: retreat to a safe, warm cave-like place. Our body heat and the physical protection it affords is the main reason why cats like to sleep on our lap. Warmth and "cave" feelings are also why the crawls under the bedcovers with you when you are in bed.

Other potential sleeping or resting sites are sun-drenched or heated window sills, in front of fireplaces, as well as all electrical appliances that radiate heat upward, e.g., TV sets. Anyone who does not want his cat in bed with him at night and wants to offer sleeping site alternatives to furniture during the day,

must offer the animal at least two attractive snug "caves." The one for nocturnal use should be on top of a closet, on a shelf, or on top of a scratching post that has a ledge on the top. The "cave" intended for brief dozing periods can be open and must afford a good, all-around view. If you have more than one cat, each must have its own special place to which it can retreat.

THE LITTER BOX

Another essential in a household with a cat is a litter box. This is where most cat owners make the most mistakes, often with irreparable consequences. In this respect, a cat is extremely sensitive; it wants to be undisturbed, feel protected, and not be irritated by other odors. Yet it also cherishes its freedom of movement. You must take all of these factors into account when selecting a litter box and deciding where you are going to keep it. The litter box should not be situated near your cat's food bowl or bed. Moreover, it should not be placed in an area that is heavily trafficked by family members. It should be large enough so that the animal can easily stand and turn around in it. Tomcats have

Purchase all of the essentials for your cat before you bring him home. One of the most important items is a litter box, which is available in a variety of designs.

a tendency to urinate in a standing position, just as they do for marking their territory. Therefore, it is advisable to provide them with a litter box with sufficiently high sides or even a domed lid. On the other hand, some female cats prefer to place their front paws at the edge of the litter box and sulk when they are offered an enclosed litter box. It might also happen that both sexes turn up their noses at an enclosed litter box because it holds the odor. Ideally, at the beginning, you should offer your kitty various alternatives and then keep the one that it prefers.

The same applies to the litter. There are many different brands available. The best known are clay and mineral pebbles. Brands that contain these tiny granules take up twice the volume of moisture and also absorb odor. These commonly used materials accommodate a cat's practice of burying its

waste materials. Another type of litter is that made from plant fibers, which has a lighter consistency than those made of the more traditional materials.

Anyone who is particularly sensitive to the odor or who owns a cat that is fussy can use one of the synthetic litters in the form of concentrate. Fill the litter box to a depth of about four to six inches, sufficiently deep so that the cat can properly cover up its feces. Even the extremely absorbent litters that form solid clumps that can be scooped out should be changed once a week. Traces of odor always remain, and a cat's nose is much more sensitive than a human's nose.

SAFETY CONSIDERATIONS FOR A CAT

Although cats that live solely indoors are exposed to fewer dangers than those that are permitted to roam freely, there are still surprisingly many accidents that can happen to your cat within your own four walls. The cause lies invariably with the insatiable curiosity of the cat.

The following list represents hazards to the curious cat: unscreened open windows, washers and dryers (cats love to curl up in warm places), self-closing doors, various kinds of houseplants (some can be poisonous), and household cleaning

products. "Cat-proofing" your home can help to prevent your cat from getting injured.

A CAT-PROOF BALCONY

Even the smallest porch or balcony is sufficient to make a little paradise for your pet. The diversity of smells, sights, and sounds offered by such places compensate a cat for its loss of freedom to roam

In warm weather, make sure that open windows are properly secured to prevent kitty from escaping.

outdoors. It is also good for the animal's health. Weather changes fortify its immune system and its fur adjusts to the change of seasons. The only problem is preventing the animal from falling off or from climbing over to adjacent balconies if you live in an apartment complex. If the landlord permits it, you can install a protective net or simply cover the outside of the balcony with wire mesh. Quite possibly, though, such a request will

Pet shops carry a wide array of cat toys that will keep your pet amused for hours on end. Photo courtesy of The Kong Company.

be denied since it has a detrimental effect on the "uniform appearance" of the building's exterior. Then you will have to come up with a clever alternative. A barred balcony railing can be covered with cloth, because the interspaces are usually wide enough for a cat to get through. A normal balcony railing height presents no problem for such an excellent jumper as a cat. But if you install 12-inch wide board along the railing, which points sharply upward, no cat will jump on it because it cannot see beyond it to find out what is on the other side. A particularly decorative solution is dense planting of climbing or creeping plants. If all of that is simply not possible, the cat must be supervised or placed in a roomy portable kennel.

A CAT-PROOF GARDEN

An escape-proof garden protects you not only from trouble with your neighbor who may not be too thrilled by cats but also makes it easier on your nerves and affords freedom for your cat. If you want to build a cat kennel within the confines of your own garden, you will need appropriate permits from your local building officials. Aviary-type structures are available from most larger pet shops and are ready to be assembled. All you have to do is to add is a scratching post and a litter box. Be sure to position the kennel in such a way that its occupant can retreat from the sun when it wants to.

Securing an entire garden is relatively simple. Tall trees close to the perimeter fence are fitted with a special wire ring (bird protection equipment) at a height of three feet. You can also employ natural climbing obstacles such as a hedge of roses or other thorny plants. This kind of "belt" prevents a cat from reaching high branches and using them as a jumping-off point to get into the neighboring property.

So that your cat can have access to the balcony, terrace, or garden when you are not at home, you can install a special cat door, which opens in both directions in response to pressure from the animal's body. There is, however, the danger that other animals may also enter your apartment.

A feather blowing about in the wind will quickly attract the attention of any cat.

TOYS

Playing is among the most elementary requirements, especially for an indoor cat. It replaces the opportunity for stalking, hunting, and prey capture. During the summer, the ever-fit cat can find prey even in the cleanest home: flies, butterflies, moths, mosquitoes, and spiders. Generally, there is little other prey to catch for a house cat. Therefore, larger "trophies" must be offered in the form of toys.

Everything that moves catches a cat's immediate attention. If it faintly resembles prey, she will stalk it, touch it briefly with her paw, and when the prey "flees," she will follow in serious, hot pursuit. However, do not be surprised if kitty quite suddenly loses interest and turns away. That too is part of a cat's normal behavior. If there is no hope of success, the hunting fever will die suddenly. Therefore, it is up to you to award a partial victory when playing this game. The cat's enthusiasm will be stirred up again, and she will thrust herself with renewed vigor at the perceived "enemy."

Apart from mobile objects, a cat is also easily intrigued by certain noises. Anything that rustles could be a mouse, and the soft chirping and humming will cause the ears of the cat to immediately perk up. You can purchase cat toys that make various animal-like noises, one of the most popular being the squeaky mouse.

Your cat will love to explore under the bedcovers, pounce on your wiggling toes, and watch in fascination when you play "ghost" with your wiggling hand concealed under a towel. Bags, baskets, and cupboards, as well as half-

Commercially prepared cat foods provide all of the essential nutrients that cats need.

open drawers, will catch your cat's attention. A simple cardboard carton, with a few holes punched into its sides, will be thoroughly inspected before the cat cautiously reaches inside of it. Some pet shops carry mouse castles, in which a ball suspended inside simulates prey. The tactile sense is stimulated by everything soft, as for instance the famous ball of wool into which every cat likes to sink its teeth! Your cat will also enjoy chasing and batting small bouncing balls.

Sometimes cat play is not all that vigorous. A cat is happy just looking through the window at some birds outside. When it watches unattainable prey, a cat will often emit "cackling" noises, during which time it will assume the jump position and excitedly whip its tail from side to side.

If there is only very little room, you can modify the scratching post into a playground: equip it with a variety of toys that are suspended by rubber bands.

DIET

The nutritional requirements of a cat are very different from those of man and other pets. She needs very little carbohydrates but a lot of protein. In the wild, roughage in the diet is provided by the pelt, bones, and skin of prey. Vitamins, trace elements, and minerals are also contained in flesh and bones. Cats

Grass is an important digestive aid for cats.

need a lot of vitamin A.. All vitamin B requirements are contained in sufficient quantities in meat, as is vitamin H (biotin), while vitamin C is produced in the body and is not taken up via food. Absolutely

Some cat owners use gloves to stroke out the dead hairs in the coat. This job can be accomplished more efficiently by using grooming tools designed for cats.

Your cat will have its ears checked as part of its regular veterinary exam.

essential is the amino acid taurine, which can not be synthesized by the cat's own body system.

Over the years, the cat food market has significantly advanced, to the point where particular cat food brands have been specially formulated to meet the precise requirements of a cat, and which can then be used exclusively for a particular animal. In addition, there are also special mixtures for kittens, adult cats, and "senior" cats. Daily energy require-ments vary, and therefore the amount of food consumed will vary also. Activity, stress, illness, and pregnancy also affect nutritional requirements.

Cut claws only up to the spot indicated; otherwise, you will cut into the "quick," the blood vessel that runs through the nail.

Tortoiseshell Persian. Longhaired breeds such as this should be groomed every day or so to keep their coats free of tangles and mats.

Cat food manufacturers provide detailed feeding instructions, which take the guesswork out of feeding your cat. A healthy cat will clearly signal when it is hungry and when it is full. Unlike dogs, cats do not feed "in advance," but instead will stop as soon as the stomach is full.

Cat food is available in three different forms: canned, dry, and semi-moist. Be sure to check the expiration date before purchase. Cat food should be stored in a cool, dry place.

Cats must have access to clean fresh water at all times. Please do not feed milk. The lactose that it contains cannot be nutri-tionally utilized by cats, and it can cause diarrhea, which then leads to an increased loss of body fluid.

GROOMING

Shorthaired breeds can be brushed every few days to remove any dead hairs. Daily brushing is absolutely essential for longhaired breeds; otherwise, the coat will become tangled and matted. It is highly advisable that grooming should be started when the animal is a kitten. Doing so will help kitty to become accustomed to the procedure by the time it is an adult.

A cat needs to be bathed only occasionally. Make sure that the room in which the bath is being given is warm and draft free. Use only a shampoo formulated especially for cats, and rinse thoroughly. Afterward, towel dry or use a hair dryer set on *low*.

HEALTH

A healthy cat has a smooth, shiny coat, clear eyes, and a clean nose. Her respiratory movements are virtually soundless, she exhibits a good appetite, and uses the litter box without vocalizing. To the

Cats that are allowed to roam freely outdoors are more prone to contract illness and disease than are those that are kept indoors.

human nose, a cat's fur is nearly odorless. The gums should have a pink color to them. If you grasp a section of neck fur with index finger and thumb, pulling it upward and then let go again, it must return to its original position (firmly around the neck) within ten seconds. The normal body temperature of a cat is between 98° and 100° F.

Cats do not complain; instead, they suffer in silence. Therefore, it is even more important that in

addition to routine veterinary examinations, you constantly look out for changes in behavior and on the body of the animal.

Clear signals that something is wrong or that a disease has taken hold are: prolonged loss of appetite, constantly regurgitating recently eaten food, a blocked nose (or nasal discharge), encrusted eyes, or eyes in which the

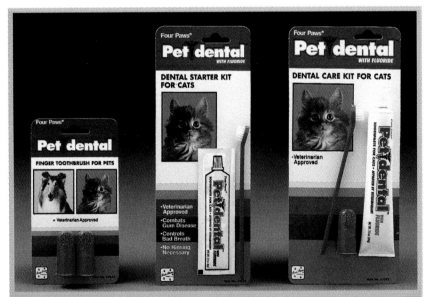

Pet dental products are available for helping to fight plaque, reduce tartar build-up, and control unpleasant breath. Photo courtesy of Four Paws.

nictitating membrane is visible. A sick cat appears apathetic. Sometimes, it crouches with tensed-up muscles at the food or water bowl; or it visits its litter box frequently. Very pale mucus membranes in the mouth, bad breath, and rough fur or

loss of hair giving rise to bare patches are also serious disease symptoms. Similarly, cats that scratch themselves constantly or slide with their anal region over the floor should be taken to a veterinarian.

Since it would go beyond the scope of this book to provide detailed descriptions of all cat diseases, only the various preventive measures will be discussed below.

DISEASE PREVENTION

With proper nutrition, maintenance of good hygiene, and meticulous grooming, the cat's own defense system is sufficiently strong to cope with small ailments like colds, gastrointestinal and circulatory disorders.

There is now a vaccine for panleukopenia. Booster shots will maintain the immunity against this formerly fatal disease. Your cat should also be vaccinated against rabies.

The dreaded cat flu complex, a disease caused by as many as three different viruses, triggered by various pathogens, is not as dangerous due to a vaccine that became available a few years ago. With an annual booster shot, you can protect your pet against this terrible disease.

With a regular triple vaccination (panleukopenia, rabies, flu) you can protect your cat against the most serious dangers. Your vet can set up a vaccination schedule for your cat.

Keep in mind that the protection of vaccinations, which cause the body to produce its own defense substances (antibodies), becomes fully effective only if the animal is in excellent physical condition at the time of vaccination. An injured cat, or one that is half starved or one that is totally worm infested must be cured *before* vaccination takes place.

WORMING

Tapeworm and roundworm infestations can not be prevented, but through regular worming you can make sure that these parasites do not

Regular veterinary care is an important part of keeping your cat healthy.

penetrate the cat's body. Suitable preparations can be prescribed by your veterinarian. If it is found that there is a serious infestation present,

This cat is being given a worming preparation. Worm infestation in cats is not unusual and can be effectively treated by a vet.

treatment can also be initiated via injections. The first worming for a kitten should take place after the 12th week.

The worm tablets can be disguised in the favorite food of your pet, and hopefully the animal will not detect them. Alternatively, you can give them directly. To do that, you open the mouth of the animal with two fingers and then push the tablet deep into the back of the throat and close the mouth again. The animal's swallowing reflex will nearly always force the tablet down.

ECTOPARASITES

Lice can really only become established on totally uncared for cats; moreover, these parasites are nowadays virtually gone from our households. On the other hand, cats are easily infested by mites,

ticks and fleas. The latter two can be combated prophylactically by the use of a parasite collar, provided that your pet tolerates the chemicals in it.

EAR MITES

These parasites can be recognized as tiny dots, or by the fact that the animal keeps shaking its head,

Because cats ingest hair when they groom themselves, they are susceptible to hair balls. There are products available that will help to relieve this problem. Photo courtesy of Four Paws.

tends to scratch a lot, and the ears seem to have become sensitive to touch. A veterinarian will treat affected ears in intervals of a few weeks and also prophylactically include all other cats on the same premises, because these

parasites are transmitted from one animal to another.

DENTAL CARE

Tooth diseases are relatively rare in cats, but gum diseases are common. Unlike a dog, a cat will not

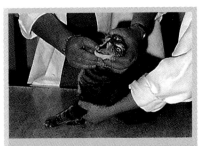

Cat health care also includes regular dental check-ups by the veterinarian.

chew for hours on an unproductive chewing bone. Dry food alone is not enough for plaque-prone animals. Once a year, possibly at the time of the annual booster-vaccination shots, the teeth and gums of your cat should be examined and any plaque should be removed. This prevents an early loss of teeth and diseases of the oral mucus membranes.

DESEXING

Anyone not planning to breed his cat should have the animal desexed after it has reached sexual maturity. For tomcats, that is usually shortly before their first birthday. For females, or queens, this is best done after the first estrus. In males, the procedure is called neutering; in females, it is referred to as spaying. Desexing your cat will not

Treats can be provided on an occasional basis to help provide a little variety in the diet. Some treats act as a cleansing agent to help reduce tartar on the cat's teeth. Photo courtesy of Heinz.

only spare you a lot of trouble but will also decrease the risk of uterine infection, which is common among unspayed females. Today, desexing is a routine surgical procedure.

YOUR CAT'S FIRST-AID KIT

Medications intended for human use, such as aspirin, can have fatal consequences for cats. Therefore, you must never experiment with medications not prescribed by a veterinarian specially for your cat. Your cat's first-aid kit should contain the following first-aid preparations: bandages, cotton, scissors, burn ointment, thermometer, tweezers, antiseptic cream or lotion, and vitamin-mineral paste.

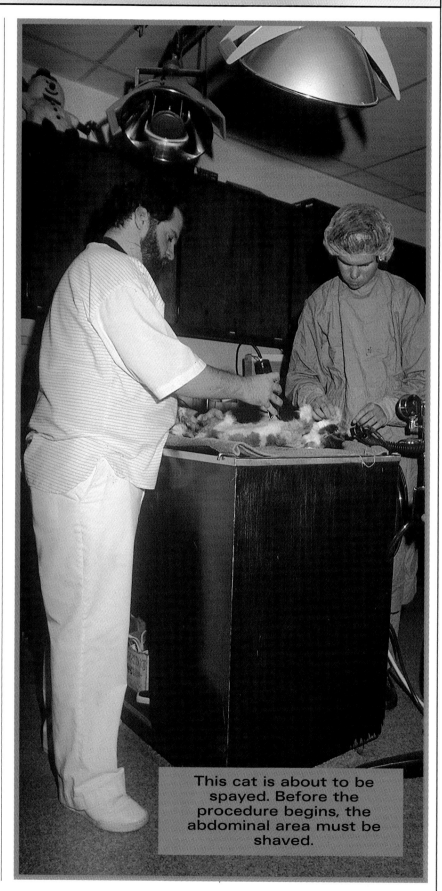

This cat is about to be spayed. Before the procedure begins, the abdominal area must be shaved.

THE PREGNANT CAT

The belief that a female cat should experience motherhood at least once in her life has caused untold harm in the history of cats. Masses of strays, wide-spread disease, drowned, poisoned kittens, and perpetually over-crowded animal shelters—all that could be avoided if appropriate cat control procedures would prevail.

Therefore, you should fully consider whether you wish to take on the responsibility for the desired cat progeny. Also keep in mind that there can be complications:

1. Cats in heat that do not mate can remain in heat for a considerable length of time because of hormonal imbalances.

2. Pregnancy is one of the factors that can cause latent diseases to become acute.

3. The birth can produce problems that may cost you time, nerves, and money.

4. The kittens will need to be vaccinated and will require veterinary care.

5. Are you sure that you will be able to find a good home for every one of the kittens?

You should also discuss your desire for kittens with your family. Only when all members agree can you go ahead in good conscience and permit your pet to become a mother.

THE CAT IN HEAT

A female cat will become sexually mature some time between the 6th and 12th month, a male after the 8th month, but it is not advisable to breed such young animals. The earliest a female should have kittens is at one year of age, because it takes that long for a proper hormonal balance to become established.

When a cat is ready to mate, she tends to throw herself to the ground, rolling ecstatically around and loudly vocalizing. This event cannot be ignored. The first time it occurs, it is triggered by an increasing length of daylight, that is, usually in February or March. In those cats that live permanently indoors, the time of year does not have any influence.

For four to ten days the female cat is highly nervous. She wants to go outside,

Thousands of cats have to be euthanized each year because there are not enough homes to go around for them. Unless you are breeding purebred show cats, you should have your cat spayed or neutered.

A female cat in heat will roll around ecstatically on the floor, loudly vocalizing at the same time.

eats only very little, and sleeps restlessly. While continuously walking around her surroundings, she rubs her head and flanks on all sorts of objects in order to give early signals to tomcats of her willingness to mate. On the third day of estrus she starts calling, mainly at night. The long, drawn-out, and loud whining, which sounds gruesome to human ears, invariably attracts tomcats, even over a long distance. The "bride" selects a number of calling places for her vocal lament.

During this period, a free-roaming female while be home only rarely, and even an apartment cat will become increasingly restless. At the peak of estrus, female cats display the typical snake-like rolling on the ground from one side over to the other. Normally by then she has attracted a whole horde of fighting (and sounding equally as gruesome) tomcats around her. But if one of them actually approaches her during the first few days of estrus, she will angrily hiss and drive him off, only to attract him again with immediately renewed purring and rolling. Only experienced tomcats will actually be able to mate with a female in heat. Young and inexperienced tomcats are allowed to practice but will be thrown off just prior to copulation.

The future father knows the fury of his bride from experience. He watches her from a safe distance and waits for two or three days of the rolling period. Following that, the female is ready to mate for a few days. She appears more benevolent and finally lets the male mount her. He grabs her firmly by the fur of the neck, and her body becomes rigid. For a few seconds she is unable to move, an interval that the male uses to copulate with her. Immediately afterward, he will escape to safety with a giant leap backward, because the female suddenly turns into a she-devil that will attack him with drawn claws and exposed teeth.

After estrus, the female regenerates her exhausted strength with extended periods of sleep and twice the normal food ration at each meal.

THE PREGNANCY

Apart from the calmer behavior of the cat, its pregnancy is not apparent during the first three weeks. The animal feeds normally, and there is no obvious change in its external appearance. After the fourth week, you can make sure whether the animal has indeed conceived. When (gently) touching the abdominal region, you can feel the hazelnut-sized heads of the embryos as if strung up on a string. Experienced cat breeders will then be able to determine the number of young they can expect. From that moment, you should avoid rough games (involving high jumps) with the pregnant animal. When lifting her up, you must use both hands, positioned forward on the animal underneath its "armpits" and in the back, below the hip joints.

From roughly about the fifth week on, you can see that the body is getting more

This pregnant queen will soon have her kittens. The gestation period in cats is between 60 to 63 days.

cylindrical and the nipples are starting to swell up. Now the cat needs twice the amount of protein, vitamins, and minerals than before.

From the seventh week of pregnancy onward, the cat grows restless; her condition has by now become obvious, and she starts looking for a nest. Those animals closely bonded to humans will nearly always select a site close to their owner—in a bed, in a wardrobe, or underneath the couch. All those places where you do *not* want your cat to drop her litter must be closed off.

As soon as the search for a nest starts, the amount of food given should be slightly reduced, and food and drink should be moved closer to the selected nest site. It is absolutely imperative that the quality of the food be maintained. You will soon discover that the female is now drinking more than usual and that she constantly changes her position while sleeping.

During the final days of her pregnancy, she is no longer able to groom herself properly, and she frequently visits her litter box. About two to three days before dropping the litter, the female's mammary line swells up further, and the teats are getting distinctly larger.

More than half of all pregnant cats drop their litter between the 63rd and 65th day after mating. In exceptional cases—in very young females, for instance—the birth of the kittens may be as early as 55 days. In females that are pregnant for the first time, the delivery may be delayed up to one week.

THE BIRTH

An imminent birth is indicated by a slight vaginal discharge, milk droplets emerging from the teats, and particularly by the behavior of the pregnant female. The animal appears very nervous, she snuggles up to you, moans softly, and ceases feeding. She keeps inspecting the nest, then leaves it again, wanders aimlessly through the house and keeps seeking contact with you. Because the kittens—about to be born—will have turned around

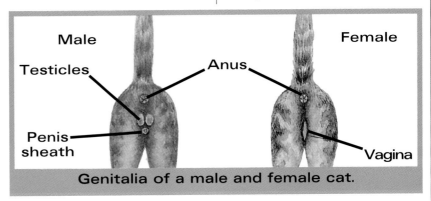
Genitalia of a male and female cat.

already, their weight presses on the bladder and intestines. That is the reason why young and inexperienced pregnant females run constantly to their litter box. These first-time mothers continue to be restless until just before the first kitten is born. The female must now be closely watched, because she may possibly drop a kitten while wandering through the house. An animal with strong human bonds will then call for you, and indeed it does not want to be alone. Gentle stroking calms the animal down and massages the body at the same time.

Cats can drop their litter in any body position, and you do not need to intervene. Do not be surprised if the future mother suddenly starts to purr. To this day it has not yet been determined whether this purring is for the still unborn kittens or whether it is a means by which the female attempts to relax herself, similar to pregnant women using breathing techniques during labor in order to relax.

Up to 24 hours can pass from the first sign of birth to the actual bearing down. But usually the first youngster appears within 12 hours after cessation of feeding.

Early labor and the bearing down stage occur simultaneously. The animal positions itself on one side, or it remains in a squatting position. The young are born in a mucus envelope, which usually tears during birth. Otherwise, the female will bite it off and then immediately lick the newborn kitten clean. In doing that, she also extracts the afterbirth by pulling on the umbilical cord before she severs the cord. Sometimes the afterbirth appears immediately after

Kitten's eyes do not open until around ten days after birth.

the birth of a kitten. In both cases, it is eaten by the female; and she also licks the amniotic fluid. In any event, you should make sure that for each kitten there is also an afterbirth.

It takes anywhere from 30 minutes to 6 hours until all the young are born, during which time you should not leave your cat alone. If the animal appears exhausted, you can offer her some lukewarm beef broth. Some cats are grateful for some protein food, given as a paste.

When you have made sure that all the young and their respective afterbirths are accounted for, and the new mother indicates with purring her acceptance of the kittens and then wants to nurse them, give her a few minutes rest. She will want to clean herself extensively, then clean her progeny, sleep for a few minutes, and then prompt her babies to feed some more.

THE KITTENS

As long as you make sure that the cat mother gets a diet of optimum quality, you do not have to worry about the well-being of the young

for the first two weeks. However, to make sure that these tiny cat babies will later turn into animals with strong affinities for people, you should make it a daily routine to pick up each kitten, stroke it gently and talk to it. It is well known that kittens treated that way will eventually form much stronger and more intimate bonds with people. From the third week on, when the youngsters are starting to walk, you should play with them and always pat them generously. That is also the time to acquaint them with other animals in the house and with other people. Their mother will teach them how to use the toilet, show them how to feed, and will take over basic training, of course, in cat style! The young kittens learn how to sharpen their claws, to threaten, to defend themselves, or to flee.

During these first few weeks, the mother will closely watch over her young around the clock. If she anticipates danger or no longer feels secure, she may move her kittens elsewhere. After three weeks—at the latest after four weeks—the kittens will take their first solid food. They are still protected against disease through immune substances in their mother's milk, so you do not have to rush with vaccinations. Only after the mother cat no longer nurses her kittens is it your turn to take over the care of the young.

The first three months in the life of a kitten represent an important phase in the development of the young animal. Mother and youngsters all interact intensely, and not everything can be replaced by humans. Therefore, the ideal time of separation is between the 12th and 14th weeks. At that point, the kittens will have learned everything that they need to know in life and by then, the mother cat becomes

Kittens are born fully furred, but they are blind and deaf. Here the queen is gently cleaning each of her youngsters.

increasingly impatient with her young.

WHAT TO DO WITH MOTHER-LESS KITTENS

Should the mother cat have died during or shortly after a difficult birth, you can attempt to rear the little ones yourself. This is possible provided that the mother was able to nurse them for at least the first 36 hours or so. During the period immediately after the birth, the colostrum contains immunoglobulin, which equips the young with antibodies against all those diseases to which the mother was exposed. There is no substitute for that milk. Consequently, kittens that miss out on it remain susceptible to disease throughout their life and usually their growth becomes adversely affected.

For rearing orphaned kittens, you should use a special preparation available from your veterinarian. It is extremely protein-rich and resembles mother's milk in its constituents. To administer this food, there are drinking bottles with rubber nipples. You must strictly adhere to the recommended amounts of food, which is dependent upon the weight of the kitten. The milk should be warmed up to about 98°F and fed six times a day during the first week. The number of meals can be reduced to five per day during the second week, and from the third week on three meals a day are sufficient. What is important, though, is that after each meal you massage the belly of the kitten with a pre-warmed hand until the youngster relieves itself. For a substitute nest, you should offer the little one a rather warm nest close to a heat source, e.g., a hot water bottle wrapped in protective material.

Because an orphaned kitten without any contact with siblings will later on display distinct behavioral disturbances, you should add either a "nurse" or another kitten.

Above: Socialization with littermates is a very important part of a kitten's development during the first three months of life. Below: Mixed breed queen and kitten. In general, mother cats are very protective of their young.

RAISING A KITTEN

No cat will respond to an order, especially not under duress. A cat's personality usually has a strongly defined self-confidence, which will only comply with its owner's desires under its own free will. Therefore, it takes certain tricks to teach the animal the essential rules of life with humans.

With a young cat this is relatively simple, because in its eyes you are taking over the mother's role. You are now the one feeding the kitten, replacing grooming with stroking, playing the protector, and the kitten watches you automatically. Because a natural (cat) mother never punishes her young, but only hisses them away or bites at them if they annoy her, young kittens do not know how to deal with punishment. Setting up a role model is the only sensible way of bringing up a kitten. With older animals that are taken in second-hand or with stray cats that may never have lived together with humans, such tricks are generally not effective. These kinds of animals have established long ago their own rules of life and will modify these rules only if they see an advantage for themselves.

In general, all animals learn from their own good as well as bad experiences, and cats are no exception. Therefore, you can proceed according to the following principle: if the cat does the correct thing, it will immediately get a reward, maybe in the form of a favorite food or some gentle stroking. If, however, the animal does something undesirable, you should scare it by throwing some noise-making object (e.g., a bunch of keys) close to it. A word of caution about such punitive measures: they must occur virtually simultaneously with the cat's action that they are intended to punish, so that there is an immediate connection in the cat's brain between these two actions. Under no circumstances must the animal become aware that it was you who scared it! Such a shock must come like a flash of lightning out of a clear blue sky. Only then will it have the desired effect.

WHAT A CAT NEEDS TO LEARN

Toilet training is among the most important things you have to teach your cat. Kittens, following their mother's example, will have learned this by the time they are four weeks old. Farmyard cats and those that have lived for a long period in kennels or animal shelters are not familiar

Cats can vary in personality, even among members of the same litter.

A cat is a very independent creature that has a mind of its own—it cannot be forced to behave in a certain way.

with a cat toilet, or they might have "forgotten" their house training. In this case, you have to watch the new cat closely, especially after extended sleeping periods and during the hour after the main meal. If you notice an indecisive walking around or you see the animal digging in a flower pot or leaving a puddle in the bathtub, you should pick up the animal and place it squarely in the litter box. Stay with the cat and praise it when indeed it uses the litter box. Never force the animal with its nose into the puddle or even into its own feces. Never grab the animal by the fur of the neck and shake it. Both of these actions are totally incomprehensible to the animal; they will only induce shyness toward humans and will not help in toilet training the animal.

To teach a cat obedience is relatively difficult. Although a cat will quickly learn to recognize its own name, because it learns that when it responds to a

certain call (its name) there is something pleasant for it, that does not mean that—like a dog—it responds to every word. You cannot force a cat to do anything, not even to accompany you. It will only do what it wants to do. It is equally pointless to expect caressing or cuddling. If the cat is not in the mood, it will perceive being kept on your lap as a physical restraint and will resist it. Sleeping sites selected by you will only be

A kitten is normally fully litter box trained by the fourth month of age, sometimes even earlier. One of the most important things that you can do to ensure that your pet uses only the litter box as a toilet is to change the litter on a regular basis.

accepted by the cat if it feels comfortable and relaxed there: it will not accept a specific sleeping basket unless it finds the basket to its liking. On the other hand, you can certainly make it clear right from the start which areas are off-limits to the cat, for instance, by locking the door to a room that it is not allowed to enter. It is

A Siamese in a state of watchful attentiveness.

important, though, that there be *no* exceptions to this rule. A cat can be extremely persistent when it wants access to a particular room. It starts with meowing, and increases to scratching and digging; it makes repeated jumps at the door handle. But this kind of behavior manifests itself only if the cat has been in that room before and liked it. To convey to the cat that it can enter the room only in your company rarely ever succeeds.

Minor misbehavior such as climbing up the curtains or stealing food from the table is handled most effectively with a spray of water or with loud hand-clapping—but only, of course, when you catch the animal in the act. Usually one or two of these scare tactics are sufficient to deter the animal from further attempts.

Although every cat resists any rigid training, most animals are willing to fit into the daily routines of a household, provided they feel comfortable with someone.

CAT BREEDS

To provide a detailed description here of all recognized breeds and their respective color varieties is clearly beyond the framework of this book. If you are interested in pedigreed cats, you should visit some of the many cat shows that are held throughout the country. They are the best places to get a comprehensive picture of the enormous diversity of cat breeds. The following is a sampling of some of the most well-known breeds of cat and their distinguishing characteristics.

Above: The British Shorthair is a medium-to-large solid cat with a massive head. In Great Britain, the breed is divided into individual breeds by color.

The American Shorthair bears a striking resemblance to the British Shorthair. The heritage of the American Shorthair goes back to the days of the pilgrims, who needed capable mousers to patrol their cabins and barns.

The Persian cat is the embodiment of grace and elegance. To keep this beautiful cat looking its best, daily grooming is a must.

Turkish Van. This breed, which originated in the Lake Van area of Turkey, is noted for its ability to swim. Vans are distinguished by their auburn-color markings.

Birman, also known as the Holy Birman and the Sacred Cat of Burma. Legends abound about the Birman, whose ancestors once graced the Buddhist temples of Burma and were revered by holy men. The Birman, whose appearance strongly suggests Siamese and Persian heritage, is distinguished by its white mitts.

Turkish Angora. This breed is derived from cats that were domesticated by the Tartars and the Chinese. It was ultimately perfected in Ankara, Turkey, thus the name Angora. Traditionally, the Angora is pure white, but it is accepted in a number of other colors.

Persian. There are now over 50 different color varieties in this breed.

PERSIAN

The cats with the longest hair are Persians, whose dense, silky coats can easily be four inches long. A thick neck fold gives these round-headed cats with the short stubby noses almost a lion-like appearance. Their eyes are a shiny emerald green or copper or orange-red, respectively. The compact body is supported by stout legs with large, round paws, which have tufts of hair between the pads. The short tail is bushy. There are now nearly fifty different color varieties of the Persian breed. This multitude is supplemented by colorpoint Persians, which have an almost completely white coat with colored patches on the limbs, tail, and on the ears and an identical face mask (nose and eye region are colored). Colorpoint Persians have blue eyes and are bred in 19 different color varieties, in which the color is restricted to the mask and the standard color patches.

Regular grooming is mandatory for these longhaired cats because they are not capable of doing it themselves. Daily combing and weekly brushing prevent the fur from becoming matted. In character, Persians are regal and serene. They do not constantly insist on playing with their owners. Their voice is very soft and pleasant. Within a family setting, they are friends with anyone.

BIRMAN

This beautiful cat is also known as the Sacred Cat of Burma. At first sight, this semi-longhaired cat looks like a colorpoint Persian.

The Birman is a gentle cat with strong affinities for people.

But the body is more slender, the head not quite as round, and the nose is slightly longer. The eggshell-colored to golden-yellow coat is in contrast to the mask, which can occur in all those colors common to colorpoint Persians. Tail, ears, and legs are all colored, but all four feet are pure white. The eyes are blue.

Birmans impress with their soft, gentle manners and their strong affinities for people. The coat does not

The Turkish Van is sometimes called "the swimming cat."

require quite as much care as that of Persians, but it should be combed and brushed regularly to prevent matting.

TURKISH VAN

This is another white, semi-longhaired cat. It has a chestnut-red tail, red patches in the face, and amber-yellow eyes, which are slightly slanted. The head is triangular, and the ears are large. The Turkish Van has semi-long fur that is easy to groom. It is alleged that this cat likes to swim and is not afraid of water. In character, it is independent yet affectionate.

The Turkish Angora has a soft, silky coat that is longest on the tail and the ruff, which is the fur that encircles the neck.

The Turkish Van is a medium-sized cat of fine bone. Males are slightly larger than females.

TURKISH ANGORA

The first Angora cats came to us from Turkey. They were also white, without any other marks. This graceful sister of the Turkish Van has blue, orange-colored, or variably colored eyes, respectively. Today, this breed is bred in many beautiful color varieties. It has a silky-soft, metallic-glistening coat and a long and tapered tail that is carried over the back when the cat is in motion. Tufts of hair on the ears and along the neck tend to give this cat a fairy-like appearance.

The Turkish Angora is an affectionate cat, one of the most sensitive among the semi-longhaired cats.

Maine Coon. This native New Englander sports a long, thick coat that protects it from the cold, harsh winters in Maine.

MAINE COON

This native New Englander is one of the largest breeds of cat. It is a powerful cat with a stunning, voluminous coat. The large ears carry tufts of hair, and the enormously large eyes give the face an owl-like appearance. The long tail

should have flowing hair. The seasonal change of fur is conspicuous: during the winter, the Maine Coon carries dense fur with a thick neck fold; during the summer, the fur is thinner.

The Maine Coon will appreciate an enclosed porch or balcony where it can safely enjoy sunshine and fresh air. Maine Coons are adept mousers. Within a family setting, they usually confine their affection only to one person.

Norwegian Forest Cat. This native of Scandinavia sports a dense, long coat that sheds as the summer months approach. The Norwegian Forest comes in a wide variety of attractive colors.

NORWEGIAN FOREST CAT

Although more delicate than the Maine Coon, this semi-longhaired cat is reminiscent of its American cousin. It has longer legs and is more slender, but it also exhibits the characteristic neck fold and the tufts of hair on the ears. Just like the Maine Coon, this cat is also being bred in different colors.

The Norwegian Forest Cat is an affectionate cat with a gentle voice and a relaxed disposition.

Somali. This longhaired version of the Abyssinian is of medium build with slender, yet sturdy, legs. The unique color markings, called ticking, enhance the overall appearance of this cat.

AMERICAN SHORTHAIR

The classic shorthaired "alley cat" of the United States is a medium to large cat with an oblong head and pronounced cheeks. The coat is thick, giving the cat plenty of protection. Colors vary, including most solids, as well as smokes,

Exotic Shorthair. The result of American Shorthair-Persian crosses, this is a cobby cat with a noticeably round head and ears that are rounded at the tips.

chinchillas, patches, bicolors, and of course tabby. The tabby American Shorthair is perhaps the most popular. The breed makes an ideal house cat,

The Somali's densely furred tail, thick at the base and tapered at the end, forms what is called a brush.

The length of the Maine Coon's coat suggests that Angora cats are probably part of its heritage.

Colors in the Norwegian Forest Cat include tabbies, solids, bi-colors, and parti-colors.

The American Shorthair is an American classic. Affable and outgoing, he is a delight to own.

loving each member of the family equally. A house with an American Shorthair has no mice!

BRITISH SHORTHAIR

From the isles of Great Britain, this miraculous shorthaired cat hails. The head of the British Shorthair is distinctive for its massiveness and circular shape. The eyes are prominent and rounded, decidedly alert. The coat is never woolly, but a resilient single coat. In color the British Shorthair is most varied, occurring in the same colors as the Persian, including chocolate, lilac and colorpoints. This Briton is hale and hearty,

British Shorthair. This hearty chap is the UK's equivalent of the American Shorthair. Medium to large in size, this breed comes in a multitude of colors.

with a lot of love and pep to share with his owners.

BENGAL

A creation of American breeder Jean Mill, this hybrid turned purebred is a strikingly beautiful spotted cat, resembling the Asian wild cat from which it is derived. The cats, long in body and substantial (males are significantly larger), can be brown spotted, marble leopard or snow leopard (silver and black rosettes

against white). Bengals can be very affectionate or somewhat aloof: both are correct and typical of the breed. These exotic cats are medium-coated, very active, endearingly primitive, and among the most handsome of all felines.

SOMALI

The agouti-patterned fur is the most conspicuous characteristic of this semi-

longhaired cat. Each individual hair has the wild coloration—it is brown, red, and blue with black bands. The eyes are amber-yellow or green with a dark margin. The Somali is slender, has long legs, and appears delicate. The large ears carry tufts of hair and have the wild spot on the outer ear. The fur is extremely dense and fine. Somalis have a strong affinity for people but can also act aloof. They normally like to play a lot.

Out of Africa into your home, this Bengal is Topspot Jafar, owned by Andrew De Prisco, showing off his fabulous pelage.

The voice is soft and is not used very often.

EXOTIC SHORTHAIR

Cobby and sturdy aptly describe the conformation of the Exotic Shorthair. This shorthaired cat has a stubby nose, small ears, and large, round eyes. The short fur is plush and dense.

These stout exotic cats are known for their peaceful and good-natured dispositions. They are very compatible with each other and with other animals.

BALINESE

The Balinese is essentially a Siamese with long hair. This cat, too, is very slender and long legged. It has large,

Balinese. The colors in this breed are the same as those in the Siamese, which was instrumental in the creation of this breed. They include seal point, chocolate point, blue point, and lilac point, which is shown here.

pointed ears and almond-shaped eyes that slant toward the nose. The fur is shiny white, with colored

Javanese. This is yet another breed whose creation is owed, in part, to the Siamese. This is readily apparent in the Javanese's overall conformation. Colors include all of those found in the Colorpoint Shorthair.

markings on the head, tail, and legs. The Balinese is a dainty cat, long and lithe in its conformation. This is also a cat with lots of temperament and enjoys its owner's company all day long.

JAVANESE

This breed combines the temperament of the Oriental with the gentleness of longhaired cats. It is very slender, with long legs, a narrow head, and a long, thin tail. In conformation, this breed is dainty and svelte. The eyes are yellow to green. All of the colors found

Chartreux. The characteristic blue-gray color of this breed can vary from light to dark. Members of this breed are sturdy and robust.

in the Colorpoint Shorthair are acceptable for the Javanese. The Javanese is easygoing, likes to play, and is very devoted to its owner.

CHARTREUX

This is a robust and athletic breed. It has a deep chest and broad shoulders. The head is round but not entirely spherical. A hallmark of the breed is the

Graceful and serene, the Russian Blue is happiest in a tranquil household. The rich blue coat and deep green eye color are the hallmarks of the breed.

slightly woolly coat, which becomes more noticeable as the cat ages. The blue-gray color can vary from light to dark.

It can be an ideal family cat, devoted to children of any age. The Chartreux is even tempered and playful.

RUSSIAN BLUE

In body structure, this cat is more delicate than the Chartreux. It is fine boned and has long, narrow legs. It is graceful in its overall appearance. The head is

The history of the European Shorthair is entwined with that of the British Shorthair. Members of this breed are down-to-earth and unassuming, an "everyman" kind of cat.

Head study of a Balinese. Note the prominently wedge-shaped head.

European Shorthair.

wedge shaped and the eyes wide set. Its most notable characteristic is the double-layered fur, which appears plush and lies smooth against the body. The Russian Blue is always blue-gray with a silver sheen, and the eyes are green. Whereas the Chartreux is for those who appreciate more relaxed cats, the Russian Blue is for fanciers of more sensitive cats.

EUROPEAN SHORTHAIR

According to the standard, the ideal

The Abyssinian bears a noticeable resemblance to the African wild cat, Felis libyca. Colors are red, blue, ruddy, and fawn, all of which are accentuated by ticking in various degrees.

European Shorthair epitomizes the good old house cat: medium large, moderately slender, well-proportioned, without any extras...but with a pedigree. The eye color can be green, yellow, orange or blue. The fur colors correspond to those of the British Shorthair.

The European Shorthair has a pleasant disposition.

The Manx originated in the Isle of Man centuries ago. As the result of a mutation, this breed is tailless: where the tail would normally begin is a hollow. Manx are friendly and affectionate cats.

In character, it is like the traditional house cat.

ABYSSINIAN

The prevailing wild coloration, or ticking, throughout characterizes the appearance of the

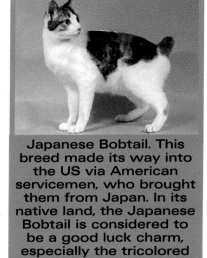

Japanese Bobtail. This breed made its way into the US via American servicemen, who brought them from Japan. In its native land, the Japanese Bobtail is considered to be a good luck charm, especially the tricolored variety.

Abyssinian. Just like the Somali, this shorthaired cat has banded hairs, a wild spot on the ear, and amber-yellow to green eyes. It is of medium size, not too

slender, but lithe.

The Abyssinian is an active, agile cat. It is self-assertive, likes to play and be cuddled, but intermittently also likes to be on its own.

MANX

The Manx developed as

Burmese. This breed sports a beautiful, satin-like coat.

the result of a mutation that occurred on the Isle of Man. As the tail is missing, this breed appears almost square in conformation. Manx cats nearly always have a slightly bent

Originating from Thailand (formerly Siam) is the silver-blue Korat. The Korat has a noticeably heart-shaped face and large, luminous green eyes.

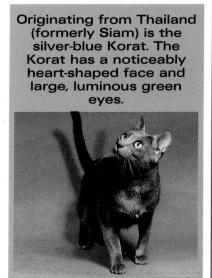

Burmese. The sable brown color, shown here, is considered by some to be the classic color for the breed.

Long, lithe, and lean aptly describe the Siamese. One of the most popular breeds, the Siamese is said to be the closest thing to a dog in a cat.

The sleek, muscular Oriental Shorthair, also called the Foreign Shorthair, comes in smoke, tabby, parti and shaded colors. Oriental Shorthairs are introspective, independent cats.

backbone. They are bred in a variety of colors.

Manx are shy but personable cats that truly enjoy the attention of members of their human family.

JAPANESE BOBTAIL

This Japanese good-luck cat is unlike the Manx. It is not totally tailless but instead has retained a bobtail. The hairs around the tip of the tail are erect so that it looks like a powder puff. The hind legs of these medium-sized cats are slightly longer than the front legs; the body is strong without appearing plump.

Bobtails are smart, inquisitive cats. They are friendly without being possessive.

Rex cats, of which there are a number of breeds, are characterized by their wavy coats. Rex cats are known for their affectionate nature and enjoy the companionship of their human family.

BURMESE

The Burmese is the energy bundle among the not- too-thin, shorthaired cats. It can not deny its relationship to the Siamese, although it deviates from it in body shape and coloration. This cat is available in a number of color varieties. It is of medium size, has a wedge-shaped head, and slanted eyes that are far apart and have a golden-yellow to amber-colored glow. The body gives an appearance of

Siamese, blue point. Siamese are very intelligent, sensitive cats.

delicateness but is muscular and compact.

The Burmese is not a cat that is content to be alone, but instead prefers to be with people. Outside access is not required, provided there are enough play opportunities in the home.

KORAT

This medium-sized cat appears somewhat cobby, with good muscle development. It has a heart-shaped face, large, prominent eyes, and a beautiful silver-blue coat of medium length.

The Korat prefers to remain elegantly reserved

Oriental Shorthair.

and is not suitable for a hectic household, although it does like to be cuddled and is an ideal house cat.

REX MUTATIONS

There are several breeds of Rex, including the Cornish Rex, Devon Rex, and German Rex., all three of which are well established. All three have a very slender body conformation, large ears, and a wedge-shaped head. The distinctive characteristic is the fur, which in the

Bengal. The Asian leopard cat was used in the creation of this breed, which displays beautiful markings in color groups known as leopard, marble leopard, and snow leopard.

Devon Rex. Members of this curly-coated breed are outgoing and playful and make great feline companions.

Cornish—particularly along the back—is curled or waved, very short, and dense. In the equally curled and wavy Devon, it is very soft and somewhat longer. In the German Rex, the hair is velvety-dense, short, and slightly wavy.

The Rex cats are very devoted pets and like to be perpetually cuddled. All three display a lot of personality and, for their delicate appearance, extraordinary power.

SIAMESE

The Siamese is a very popular breed of cat. It is a slender animal with tall legs, a long and narrow head, large ears, and almond-shaped, vivid blue eyes. The body is ivory colored, with the characteristic markings common to all masked cats.

Among all pedigreed cats, the Siamese is considered to be the one with the strongest affection for humans. It adores its human master. In terms of temperament, Siamese cats cannot be compared to any other breed. They are always active, playing wildly and enthusiastically. They like to cuddle and are very compassionate. A bundle of energy, the Siamese is totally devoted to its owner, but expects similar devotion in return.

ORIENTAL SHORTHAIR

This breed is slender and long, with fine musculature. The ears are large and pointed and complete the appearance of the wedge-shaped head. The medium-sized eyes are almond shaped.

These cats display the same affinities for play and devotion to humans as their masked sisters. They are not for people who like to have peace in the evening. Instead, they need people around them who really enjoy a cat's company.

T.F.H. offers the most comprehensive collection of books dealing with cats. A selection of significant titles is presented below; they and many other works are available from your local pet shop.

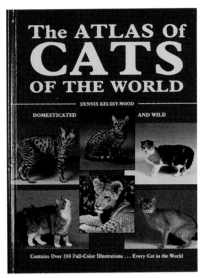

TS-127, 384 pages
over 350 full-color
photos

TS-173, 304 pages
over 400 full-color
photos

TS-253, 320 pages
over 230 full-color
photos

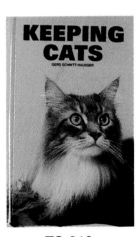

TS-219,
192 pages
over 90
full-color
photos

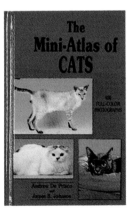

TS-152,
448 pages
over 400
full-color
photos

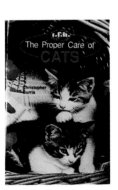

TW-103,
256 pages
over 200
full-color
photos